I Build a Lighted House
& Therein Dwell:

Love in Action

Susan MacNeil, Ph.D.

Limits of Liability and Disclaimer of Warranty

The author/publisher shall not be liable for your misuse of this material. This book is strictly for informational and educational purposes.

Warning – Disclaimer

The purpose of this book is to educate and entertain. It is distributed with the understanding that the publisher is not engaged in the dispensation of legal, psychological or any other professional advice. The content of each entry is the expression and opinion of its author and does not necessarily reflect the beliefs, practices or viewpoints of the publisher, its parent company or its affiliates. The publisher's choice to include any material within is not intended to express or imply any warranties or guarantees of any kind. The author and/or publisher do not guarantee that anyone following these techniques, suggestions, tips, ideas, or strategies will become successful. The author and/or publisher shall have neither liability nor responsibility to anyone with respect to any loss or damage caused, or alleged to be caused, directly or indirectly, by the information contained in this book.

Cover photo is of the Temple at Christ College of Trans-Himalayan Wisdom, Southern Lights Centre, New Zealand. Used with permission.

The title refers to the spiritual/soul keynote for the sign of Cancer published in *Esoteric Astrology* by Alice A. Bailey.

ISBN 13: 978-1984137494
ISBN 10: 1984137492

Finding inspiration for yourself in this book?

I'd love to hear about it!

Please email me at SusanMacNeilphd@gmail.com

or visit my website at www.PsychologywithaSoul.com.

About the Author

Dr. Susan MacNeil earned her Ph.D. in clinical psychology and is a licensed Mental Health Counselor and Board Certified Coach specializing in psychotherapy with individuals, couples and groups. A variety of issues that Dr. MacNeil commonly deals with are trauma, including childhood trauma, depression and feelings of emptiness, anxiety (fear & worry), including death anxiety and performance anxiety, loss, women's issues, spiritual and midlife crises, and career changes. She brings her expertise from the past 25 years of psychotherapy practice and strives to adapt her work to each person by employing established and innovative methods such as: psychodynamic psychotherapy, transpersonal & positive psychology, relational psychoanalysis, psychosynthesis, cognitive techniques, EMDR, and psychodrama. Her background and proficiency as a martial artist, dance therapist, and performance artist, similarly enlighten her work.

Her specialties include:

- Relationship Therapy
- Couples Counseling
- Spiritual Crisis
- EMDR
- Creative Meditation
- Trauma
- Artists' Issues
- Group Therapy
- Loss & Grief

- Life Coaching
- Health & Family Issues

Dr. MacNeil enjoys characterizing her practice as *Psychology with a Soul*, since she has been a long-time student of the Ageless Wisdom philosophy incorporating Eastern and Western traditions. She has experienced that the system of Raja Yoga, known as the Yoga of the Mind, or the Science of the Soul, informs her practice on the deepest curative levels.

Her independent study of esoteric literature since the mid 1970s has facilitated her many publications and presentations. She appears alongside Lama Surya Das, Robert Thurman and Ervin Laszlo as one of the "World's leading psychological and spiritual experts..." in several PBS documentaries, including: *Love*; *Overcoming the Dark Side*; *Wake Up and Get Healthy*; and *Happiness* (all produced by Gary Null Productions).

She is affiliated with the non-governmental organization, the Aquarian Age Community (AAC) headquartered at the United Nations, and has presented at the UN on various topics relating to the goal of the AAC, which is to facilitate and strengthen the spiritual work of the UN.

About Dr. MacNeil's Services

Psychology with a Soul perceives psychological difficulties as universal to the human experience. While the psychological field commonly subdivides psychological manifestations in more pathological terms, *Psychology with a Soul* is a more holistic approach to psychological wellness and living. Along with established and innovative methods of psychology, *Psychology with a Soul* includes a spiritual dimension by incorporating operational links to the soul or Intuitive nature. The nature of the soul is relationship.

Facing and overcoming psychological crises is a process of increasing awareness of the duality (Spirit vs. matter) and the triplicity (physical, emotional, mental) of our human nature. The first step is to address the healing needed within these three aspects, which makes way for the full integration of all aspects of our nature. Without the ability to be the "detached observer" of our emotional states, actions, and reactions (which correspond with psychological concepts such as the development of an "observing ego," mentalizing, and mindfulness), we cannot begin to resolve emotional conflicts or integrate our emotional and mental natures.

There are a number of methods or techniques that help individuals to center themselves and become open to their higher nature. This in turn allows them to focus on their needs, wishes and goals. I choose the methods I think will work best with my clients in helping them entertain new thoughts and feelings on their intuitive journey.

My practice includes classic psychodynamic explorations of individual development as well as all familial relationships, and psychotherapeutic tools such as EMDR, psychodrama techniques and creative meditation. I will demonstrate the use of these tools later with client examples.

Note from the Author

The theme for this book, *I Build a Lighted House and Therein Dwell*, has a few stories. But all start with one thing: Love in Action. The first story of Love in Action is accomplished through self-love and self-care. Putting yourself first is necessary for loving others and making your mark here on Earth. The second story is about bringing your Soul consciousness/mindfulness in alignment with love. It is the synthesis of the head (active intelligence) and the heart (love). The third story is about Universal love, your relationship to the world, and blossoming forth in that world.

I work with many clients who have experienced trauma in life. It is not what all clinicians choose to work with; however, it is where my gifts are called. I am able to bring together what is separated in them. I blend the psychological (intellectual and emotional) with the spiritual in this integrative healing process. It may seem that the light or spark of the soul is just not there, but that is not so. It is merely turned down so low that it can't be felt or seen. In our integrative work we prepare and condition the house (the personality) to receive illumination from the Soul.

Dr. Susan MacNeil

Section One:
Self-Love

Self-love doesn't come easy to a lot of people, as they are used to putting themselves last: physically, emotionally and spiritually. It can feel like an indulgence or even selfish. Within the healing professions, however, the notion of self-love is universally recognized as foundational. If one has been sufficiently loved then extending this to the self in the form of self-care/self-love is a natural process.

Self-love creates good health (meaning integrating one's physical, emotional and mental well-being). If this is disrupted, symptoms of illness are a sign that balance needs to be restored so the healthy flow of universal intelligence can be reestablished.

This balance starts in the mind and with what you think about, because the body follows the mind. You may be familiar with how stressful thoughts may lead to tight neck muscles, headaches, and sleeplessness. At the same time, if you make a conscious effort to think more positively and develop healthy coping mechanisms, your body will reflect that too. Another way to look at it is to take a break from self-judgment and be more kind to yourself.

How do you do this? One way is by noticing your physical and emotional needs. What is it that will make you happy and healthy? Another way is to practice a healthy mindset on a daily basis. This isn't a sugar coating of everything. Instead it's about getting in alignment with what's right in the world—and in your life. This is what being mindful is all about. When you bring awareness to your thoughts, feelings and body sensations, you're being mindful—and research says you are actually remodeling the physical structure of your brain. My philosophy is you are remodeling the structure of your life!

Here are two stories of "self" love that demonstrate what is possible when recognition dawns that you are worthy and others are here to help...

Barbara's Story of Light

Barbara was an extraordinarily talented and gifted individual who came from a family afflicted with mental illness, which tested the bounds of what is commonly referred to as "reality." She had been unconsciously testing her living hypothesis about the world based upon this template of her family: Is what is true in the microcosm (my family) also true in the macrocosm (the world of people)? In her family there was no commonly held or consistent truth nor story nor roles nor expectations nor experience—it was all fluid.

This client was living the same challenges through all her relationships just as her family had challenged and tested her. By doing this, she faced difficult relationships in general, and especially at work.

After finding out more about Barbara and what plagued her, we began a vital two-fold treatment of group and individual psychotherapy. Group work was especially important for helping her orient to a functional family experience with a single verifiable "reality" in which trust was possible. While individual treatment followed traditional psychodynamic explorations of her troubled relationships, we additionally employed the use of EMDR as a tool for more securely revisiting the traumatic exchanges of her past in search of the real versus the unreal.

Barbara defined her own reality further through a safe and loving context, which helped her accept herself as lovable. At the end of her therapy, Barbara was able to experience self-love and love and respect for others through relationship.

Jane's Story of Heart

Jane was filled with fear and hate from a childhood of loss, grief, abuse, pain and suffering. I saw her three times a week and had established a trusting bond—enough to express her shadow side that enabled her to become that hateful person she believed she was.

For five months she came in and expressed high levels of rage, she demeaned and devalued the therapeutic process.

I used every method of my training to try to achieve a balance for healing: analysis, identifying with the aggressor, inner child archetype work, even joining her rage, slapping my chair and saying, "Everyone has their limits of abuse; this is mine."

It was tough for me. I felt like a fraud. Sometimes I felt like my brain was sweating. But I kept trying.

The next day she came and was as loud and abusive as ever. While sitting quietly, without attempting to "do" anything, I felt a shift toward an "experience near position" occur and began weeping uncontrollably. She stopped. She stared. She asked, "Why are you crying?" I said, "I'm feeling so sad for you, afraid and alone. My heart is aching."

Linking with a higher level, "the Soul," allowed me to join Jane through loving sympathy, through compassion, through tears. I was able to witness and recognize her pain and sadness, an experience we fumblingly give the term of acceptance.

Our relationship and her life took a major turn. Through the experience of a loving attachment and a shared emotional experience, she was able to use her mind and heart together to pull out of the emotional center. It takes courage to change, especially in the face of fear. Being with the pain of "aloneness" and opening the heart were the steps ahead for her.

Quotations About Self Love

"Love yourself first
and everything else falls into line.
You really have to love yourself to
get anything done in this world."

~ Lucille Ball

"You yourself,
as much as anybody in the entire universe,
deserve your love and affection."

~ Buddha

"When you adopt the viewpoint that there is nothing that exists that is not part of you, that there is no one who exists who is not part of you, that any judgment you make is self-judgment, that any criticism you level is self-criticism, you will wisely extend to yourself an unconditional love that will be the light of the world."

~ *Harry Palmer*

"Until you value yourself,
you won't value your time.
Until you value your time,
you will not do anything with it."

~ *M. Scott Peck*

"To love oneself is
the beginning of a life-long romance."

~ *Oscar Wilde*

"A man cannot be comfortable without
his own approval."

~ *Mark Twain*

"Remember always that you not only have
the right to be an individual,
you have an obligation to be one."

~ *Eleanor Roosevelt*

"Self-care is never a selfish act—it is simply
good stewardship of the only gift
I have, the gift I was put on earth
to offer to others."

~ *Parker Palmer*

"If only you could sense how important you
are to the lives of those you meet;
how important you can be to people you
may never even dream of.
There is something of yourself that you
leave at every meeting with
another person."

~ *Fred Rogers*

"Never be bullied into silence.
Never allow yourself to be made a victim.
Accept no one's definition of your life,
but define yourself."

~ *Harvey Fierstein*

"When you recover or discover something
that nourishes your soul and brings joy,
care enough about yourself
to make room for it in your life."

~ *Jean Shinoda Bolen*

"What lies behind us and
what lies before us
are tiny matters compared to
what lies within us."

~ Ralph Waldo Emerson

"You have been criticizing yourself
for years, and it hasn't worked.
Try approving of yourself and
see what happens."

~ Louise L. Hay

"A healthy self-love means we have no
compulsion to justify to ourselves
or others why we take vacations,
why we sleep late, why we buy new shoes,
why we spoil ourselves from time to time.
We feel comfortable doing things which
add quality and beauty to life."

~ Andrew Matthews

"You are very powerful, provided you know how powerful you are."

~ *Yogi Bhajan*

"There are days I drop words of comfort on myself like falling leaves and remember that it is enough to be taken care of by myself."

~ *Brian Andreas*

"There is nothing noble about being superior to some other man.
The true nobility is in being superior to your previous self."

~ *Hindu Proverb*

"Don't rely on someone else for your happiness and self-worth. Only you can be responsible for that. If you can't love and respect yourself, no one else will be able to make that happen. Accept who you are—completely; the good and the bad—and make changes as YOU see fit—not because you think someone else wants you to be different."

~ *Stacey Charter*

"It ain't what they call you,
it's what you answer to."

~ W.C. Fields

"I found in my research that the
biggest reason people aren't more self-
compassionate is that they are afraid they'll
become self-indulgent. They believe self-
criticism is what keeps them in line.
Most people have gotten it wrong because
our culture says being hard on yourself is
the way to be."

~ Kristen Neff

"Your problem is you're…too busy holding onto your unworthiness."

~ *Ram Dass*

"People are like stained-glass windows. They sparkle and shine when the sun is out, but when the darkness sets in their true beauty is revealed only if there is light from within."

~ *Elisabeth Kübler-Ross*

"Most of the shadows of this life
are caused by standing in
one's own sunshine."

~ *Ralph Waldo Emerson*

"When I loved myself enough, I began
leaving whatever wasn't healthy. This
meant people, jobs, my own beliefs and
habits—anything that kept me small.
My judgment called it disloyal.
Now I see it as self-loving."

~ Kim McMillen

"It took me a long time not to judge myself
through someone else's eyes."

~ Sally Field

"There came a time when the risk to remain tight in the bud was more painful than the risk it took to blossom."

~ *Anaïs Nin*

"The best day of your life is the one on which you decide your life is your own. No apologies or excuses. No one to lean on, rely on, or blame. The gift is yours—it is an amazing journey—and you alone are responsible for the quality of it. This is the day your life really begins."

~ *Bob Moawad*

"Sometimes life is living
with your heart outside of your body."

~ *President Barak Obama*

"You're always with yourself, so you might
as well enjoy the company."

~ *Diane Von Furstenberg*

"The better you feel about yourself,
the less you feel the need to show off."

~ *Robert Hand*

"You must do the thing you think you
cannot do."

~ *Eleanor Roosevelt*

"When we are no longer able to change a situation…we are challenged to change ourselves."

~ *Victor Frankl*

"Follow the three R's:
Respect for self;
Respect for others, and
Responsibility for all your actions."

~ *Dalai Lama*

"It's surprising how many persons go through life without ever recognizing that their feelings toward other people are largely determined by their feelings toward themselves, and if you're not comfortable within yourself, you can't be comfortable with others."

~ Sidney J. Harris

"By failing to prepare, you prepare to fail."

~ Benjamin Franklin

"Our deepest fear is not that we are inadequate. Our deepest fear is that we are powerful beyond measure. It is our light, not our darkness that most frightens us."

~ Marianne Williamson

"Life isn't about finding yourself. Life is about creating yourself."

~ George Bernard Shaw

"To establish true self-esteem
we must concentrate on our successes
and forget about the failures and the
negatives in our lives."

~ *Denis Waitley*

"If I cannot do great things, I can do small things in a great way."

~ *Martin Luther King*

"I think everybody's weird. We should all celebrate our individuality and not be embarrassed or ashamed of it."

~ *Johnny Depp*

"Trust yourself. You know more than you think you do."

~ *Benjamin Spock*

"Low self-esteem is like driving through life with your hand-break on."

~ *Maxwell Maltz*

"If you aren't good at loving yourself, you will have a difficult time loving anyone, since you'll resent the time and energy you give another person that you aren't even giving to yourself."

~ *Barbara De Angelis*

"Our self-respect tracks our choices. Every time we act in harmony with our authentic self and our heart, we earn our respect. It is that simple. Every choice matters."

~ *Dan Coppersmith*

"Do your thing and don't care if they like it."
~ Tina Fey

"The reward for conformity is that everyone likes you but yourself."

~ Rita Mae Brown

"Live your questions now, and perhaps even without knowing it, you will live along some distant day into your answers."

~ *Rainer Maria Rilke*

"A dreamer is one who can only find his way by moonlight, and his punishment is that he sees the dawn before the rest of the world."

~ *Oscar Wilde*

"She lacks confidence, she craves admiration insatiably. She lives on the reflections of herself in the eyes of others. She does not dare to be herself."

~ Anais Nin

"Self-pity gets you nowhere. One must have the adventurous daring to accept oneself as a bundle of possibilities and undertake the most interesting game in the world making the most of one's best."

~ Harry Emerson Fosdick

"To be beautiful means to be yourself. You don't need to be accepted by others. You need to accept yourself."

~ *Thich Nhat Hanh*

"People will suffer almost anything as long as it means they don't have to change."

~ *Deepak Chopra*

"It is cheerful to God when you rejoice or laugh from the bottom of your heart."

~ *Martin Luther King*

"It is never too late to be what you might have been."

~ *George Eliot*

"Because one believes in oneself, one doesn't try to convince others. Because one is content with oneself, one doesn't need others' approval. Because one accepts oneself, the whole world accepts him or her."

~ *Lao-Tzu*

Section Two:
Soul Love

The Soul is an entity, substance, essence or the cause of individual life. Separate from the body, it is psychical in nature, where it resides in a higher plane. It isn't the mind, but it thinks and "wills." The soul serves as the mediator between the personality and Spirit. It animates the body and is the principle of passion.

Aristotle said, "The soul is to the body what vision is to the eye." Alice Bailey says, "The Soul is the quality which every form manifests...and makes one [person] different from another in appearance, nature or character."

I believe the purpose of spiritual science is to bring us into relationship with the soul. Whereas self-care is the physical, emotional and mental well-being of an integrated personality, soul-care is awakening the intuition, another level of consciousness, through meditation, living consciously, and actively bridging the head (intelligence) and the heart (love).

When you think about it, everything is related to love—as the song goes, "love is all there is." But it doesn't come naturally, it must be practiced. It is a lifting from the integrated personality to the higher realm, where it resonates with the soul nature. To practice means to lift your thoughts to the Light. It means building a relationship between the soul and other people.

The soul is, of course, related to intuition. It's related to the coincidences, synchronicities, and intuitive voices that we all have. It allows us to be aware of higher impressions. Everything is connected—the mind, the body, and the environment. We are inseparable from it all—and it all lives in an infinite field of intelligence.

Here is an example of "Soul" love and how it manifests in everyday life...

Luke's Story of Love

Luke came in with complicated grief and loss. He also was burdened with the view of himself held by others. He felt he was not allowed to have his own story and others' stories were projected onto him. There was an additional burden that if he did not accept these false stories, he would face rejection by his family.

Phase 1: Securing the Attachment

In the wake of such a breach of trust, the formulation of a trust and alliance was essential in forming a secure attachment. Without a secure attachment it was not possible for Luke to internalize a therapeutic relationship that could demonstrate placing his inner well-being above another's. We were looking for a way to allow himself to actively challenge and question and not just passively accept what others said.

Phase 2: Releasing the Grief and Loss

In our work together, Luke and I began by allowing his grief to find expression and be processed on all levels: physical, emotional, and spiritual. This included exploring and understanding why he felt his family needed to deny the truth of his story and why he thought they attempted to devalue him as a way of silencing his truth.

Phase 3: Challenging Familial Belief System

The use of the method of EMDR helped Luke let go of his role by slowing things down and making more space in his life. Although it seemed he was being scapegoated, a part of him believed all these projections were true. Through this process we were able to challenge this belief system of the projections that he was the disruptive element of the family. The use of EMDR began the process of mindful exploration and opened the narrative to the possibility of all the additional truths of his experience.

Before Luke had only believed he could experience love through devotion. He felt he owed something to these people in his life. He had to work through strong feelings of anger and resentment to reach a higher place of loving without obligation, of caring without resentment, of giving of himself without expectation. He arrived at this new position of loving on his own terms, through his own discovery and experience of right relationship to self. He was then able to extend this right human relationship to others. Not because they'd earned or deserved this love, but because of abundant love of self, he now had abundant love to give. He had found his personal power through love.

Quotations About Soul Love
(Mindfulness)

"He said, 'You become. It takes a long time. That's why it doesn't happen often to people who break easily, or have sharp edges, or who have to be carefully kept. Generally, by the time you are Real, most of your hair has been loved off, and your eyes drop out and you get loose in the joints and very shabby. But these things don't matter at all, because once you are Real you can't be ugly, except to people who don't understand.'"

~ *The Velveteen Rabbit*

"Where the spirit does not work with the hand there is no art."

~ Leonardo Da Vinci

"You in others, this is your Soul."

~ Russian poet Pasternak

"Sorrow sweeps clean the house so joy may move in."

~ Rumi

"In solitude the rose of the soul flourishes; in solitude the divine self can speak; in solitude the faculties and graces of the higher self can take root and blossom."

~ *Alice A. Bailey*

"All that we are arises with our thoughts. With our thoughts, we make the world."

~ Buddha

"Take into account that great love and great achievements involve great risk."

~ Dalai Lama

"Who looks outside, dreams; who looks inside, awakes."

~ *Carl Gustav Jung*

"Guided by my heritage of a love of beauty and a respect for strength—in search of my mother's garden, I found my own."

~ *Alice Walker*

"We can chart our future clearly and wisely only when we know the path which has led to the present."

~ *Adlai E. Stevenson*

"Solitude is the best friend of achievement, but sometimes witnesses are needed."

~ *Agni Yoga Teaching*

"In the end, just three things matter: How well we have lived. How well we have loved. How well we have learned to let go."

~ *Jack Kornfield*

"Be joyful, for joy lets in the light, and where there is joy there is little room for… misunderstanding."

~ *Alice A. Bailey*

"In today's rush, we all think too much—seek too much—want too much—and forget about the joy of just being."

~ *Eckhart Tolle*

"The best way to capture moments is to pay attention. This is how we cultivate mindfulness. Mindfulness means being awake. It means knowing what you are doing."

~ *Jon Kabat-Zinn*

"Peace is the state where love abides and seeks to share itself."

~ *Mahatma Gandhi*

"Love, enjoyed by the ignorant, becomes bondage. The very same love, tasted by one with understanding, brings liberation."

~ *Aryadeva*

"The hidden harmony is stronger than the visible."

~ *Heraclitus*

"The light of the soul is like an immense searchlight, the beams of which can be turned in many directions, and focused on many levels."

~ *Alice A. Bailey*

"Remember that silence is sometimes the best answer."

~ *Dalai Lama*

"Forgiveness is the fragrance from the violet beneath the heel which has crushed it."

~ *Mark Twain*

"He who said, 'love one another,' was a true Yogi. Therefore…welcome each outburst of love and self-sacrifice."

~ *Agni Yoga Teaching*

"For it is in the giving that we receive."

~ *St. Francis of Assisi*

"…the sole purpose is to provide infinite springs, at which the soul may allay the eternal thirst TO KNOW which is forever unquenchable within it, since to quench it, would be to extinguish the soul's self…"

~ *Edgar Allan Poe*

"Not to be loved is miserable,
but not to love is catastrophe."

~ Rip Taylor

"The world is not falling apart, the veil of
world-wide corruption is lifting."

~ Unknown

"Let us accept love as the motive force in the expansion of consciousness. The heart will not be aflame without love; it will not be invincible, nor will it be self-sacrificing. So let us bring gratitude to every receptacle of love, for love lies on the border of the new world, where hatred and intolerance have been abolished."

~ *Agni Yoga Teaching*

"If you cannot turn the wind,
turn your sails."

~ *Secretary General Ban Ki Moon*

"If you want others to be happy, practice
compassion. If you want to be happy,
practice compassion."

~ *Dalai Lama*

"Mindfulness is simply being aware of what is happening right now without wishing it were different; enjoying the pleasant without holding on when it changes (which it will); being with the unpleasant without fearing it will always be this way (which it won't)."

~ *James Baraz*

"It's only when we truly know and understand that we have a limited time on earth and that we have no way of knowing when our time is up that we will begin to live each day to the fullest, as if it was the only one we had."

~ *Elisabeth Kübler-Ross*

"Imagination is more important
than knowledge."

~ *Albert Einstein*

"Follow your bliss. Find where it is and don't be afraid to follow it."

~ *Joseph Campbell*

"In its essence, the heart is an organ of higher action and giving;
that is why every act of giving partakes of the nature of the heart."

~ *Agni Yoga Teaching*

"Love one another but make not a bond of love, let there be a moving sea between the shores of your souls.
Sing and dance together and be joyous, but let each one of you be alone."

~ *Kahlil Gibran*

"If we learn to open our hearts, anyone, including the people who drive us crazy, can be our teacher."

~ *Pema Chodron*

"Feelings come and go like clouds in a windy sky. Conscious breathing is my anchor."

~*Thich Nhat Hanh*

"Everybody can be great…because anybody can serve. You only need a heart full of grace. A soul generated by love."

~ Martin Luther King

"If you want to conquer the anxiety of life, live in the moment, live in the breath."

~ Amit Ray

"Suffering usually relates to wanting things to be different than they are."

~ *Allan Lokos*

"In this moment, there is plenty of time. In this moment, you are precisely as you should be. In this moment, there is infinite possibility."

~ *Victoria Moran*

"Everything is created twice, first in the mind and then in reality."

~ *Robin S. Sharma*

"Don't believe everything you think. Thoughts are just that—thoughts."

~ *Allan Lokos*

"Respond; don't react. Listen; don't talk. Think; don't assume."

~ *Raji Lukkoor*

"Do every act of your life as though it were the last act of your life."

~ *Marcus Aurelius*

"What matters most is how well you walk through the fire."

~ *Charles Bukowski*

"I love it when the fire of love radiates so much that one can overcome any obstacle!"

~ *Agni Yoga Teaching*

Section Three:

Universal Love & Life Purpose

Universal love is often experienced in relationship to the world and through blossoming forth in that world. This can manifest through roles of service, which composes our life purpose.

As much as we wish, our life purpose doesn't just drop into our laps one day. It's not something we "think up" either. Instead it's something the mind, heart and Soul reveal to us. It's like a treasure we unearth as we live our lives. That is, if we keep our eyes and ears and hearts and minds open.

Many times people focus on something they want or think or believe their life purpose to be. But what if it's not something we figure out and, like said above, something that's discovered by us? How do we go about that? We go about that by experimenting, experiencing and expressing.

We start by taking steps toward what we want, and removing those things in our lives that we don't want. Take action and start attempting the things related to what we think our life's purpose could be. Teach the class. Paint the canvas. Apply for the position. Don't listen to the part of us that questions our self and instead focus on doing. Let's see what the experience brings us. Our actions will lead to clarity and we'll recognize right away if these actions are a good fit for us. If they are, great—keep going. If they're not, try something else. The journey is the process and the reward.

Remember that the key is love. We each must ask ourselves, "What do I love?" and notice when we are inspired, joyful and in the flow. We must pay attention to the insights we gain as we journey through our lives, and remember that we may have more than one purpose. Our purpose can be parenting, coaching, teaching, speaking, writing, and more. Each one of these roles can be fulfilling in its own way, as well as connect us to each other and to the Universal sense of oneness.

Here are two stories demonstrating what happens when a person discovers life purpose and universal love...

Jonathan's Story of Worth

I worked with Jonathan to help him with the frustration of not knowing his purpose in life and how to find his "worth." He worked for a large corporation and was making money, which was one of his desires, and was making his way up the corporate ladder, but he felt he was "selling his soul."

He didn't believe that the methods of treating workers and the outsourcing practices the corporation had started were fair. In our work together, this client realized he was in the wrong place and studying the wrong thing. He went back to school to become a therapist because he realized he wanted to help those who were suffering in mind and spirit.

Today he is successful and pursuing his dreams in these areas.

It is important that this client identified something in him that was restless and not feeling in alignment with who and what he really believed. He also had a strong reaction to what he perceived as injustice, which caused him to seek me out. I'm so glad he did!

Sarah's Story of Purpose and How Crisis Awakens the Soul

Sarah was a highly successful, multi-talented, and tenderhearted woman who seemed to have it all. But she felt something was amiss because she had never dealt with some devastating childhood trauma.

Although loved and admired by those who had experienced her gifts, she had not been, in her personal house of relationships, valued and validated. She had achieved a mind/heart alignment, and her Soul was prevalent in her work, however, her sense of purpose was lost. She was operating at a Soul level that had never been authenticated by her closest relationships. She was experiencing a spiritual crisis.

Her personality vehicle, by contrast with her soul vehicle, felt dim and flat. We explored her history of pain, loss, abuse and confusion through her memories and stories using EMDR and psychodrama, and we integrated spiritual techniques such as meditations, visualizations, "As If," and spiritual readings." We avoided "spiritual bypassing" by integrating her painful history through understanding how it was playing out in Sarah's present relationships.

Purpose is the final alignment for the deliverance of the Soul. This was what Sarah was striving for. Her Soul energy was matched by integrating the recharged energy of her personality. True joy was gained in her personal life. Sarah had become a diamond under the pressure of integrating her personality's and Soul's purpose.

Quotations About
Universal Love & Life Purpose

"In order to develop love—universal love, cosmic love, whatever you would like to call it—one must accept the whole situation of life as it is, both the light and the dark, the good and the bad. One must open oneself to life, communicate with it."

~ *Chogyam Trungpa*

"Act as if what you do makes a difference. It does."

~ *William James*

"We are all meant to shine, as children do. We were born to make manifest the glory of God that is within us. It is not just in some of us; it is in everyone and as we let our own light shine, we unconsciously give others permission to do the same. As we are liberated from our own fear, our presence automatically liberates others."

~ *Marianne Williamson*

"Didn't it go by awfully fast?"

~ *Howard Austen*
(Gore Vidal's partner, on his deathbed.)

"Too many people overvalue what they are
not and undervalue what they are."

~ *Malcolm S. Forbes*

"Don't ask yourself what the world needs, ask yourself what makes you come alive. And then go and do that. Because what the world needs is people who have come alive."

~ *Howard Washington Thurman*

"Meditation [upon] nature, Meditation upon quality, Meditation upon purpose, Meditation upon the soul, through these four stages of meditation the aspirant arrives at their goal, knowledge of the soul, and of the soul powers."

~ Alice A. Bailey

"No one can make you feel inferior without your consent."

~ Eleanor Roosevelt

"Whatever course you decide upon,
there is always someone to tell you
that you are wrong.
There are always difficulties arising
which tempt you to believe that
your critics are right.
To map out a course of action
and follow it to an end requires courage."

~ *Ralph Waldo Emerson*

"Never bend your head. Always hold it high. Look the world straight in the face."

~ *Helen Keller*

"Be faithful to that which exists within yourself."

~ *André Gide*

"May we live in peace without weeping. May our joy outline the lives we touch without ceasing. And may our love fill the world, angel wings tenderly beating."

~ *An Irish Blessing*

"Today is a good day for good thoughts."

~ *Agni Yoga Teaching*

"To see with the eyes of the heart; to hear the roar of the world with the ears of the heart; to peer into the future with the understanding of the heart; to remember past accumulations through the heart— that is how the aspirant must boldly advance on the path of ascent."

~ *Agni Yoga Teaching*

"You cannot perceive beauty
but with a serene mind."

~ Henry David Thoreau

"If you ask me what I came to do in this
world, I, an artist, will answer:
I am here to live out loud."

~ Émile Zola

"When we do align with it, we thrive. And when we do not, we suffer. This is not 'punishment.' It is merely the Law of Cause and Effect. With each thought we think, we either align with universal love, or we disconnect ourselves from it. Whichever is our choice determines whether we then feel connected to, or disconnected from, our own true Selves."

~ *Marianne Williamson*

"Share your knowledge. It's a way to achieve immortality."

~ *Dalai Lama*

"As I look at what's going on in the world right now in a sense it really is a reflection of what's going on within me.
Wars and uprisings are popping up everywhere and sure as hell I have my own inner war of love versus fear."

~ *A private patient*

"There is turmoil under the heavens.
The prospects are excellent."

~ Mao Tse Tsung

"It is not our purpose to become each
other; it is to recognize each other,
to learn to see the other and honor him
for what he is."

~ Hermann Hesse

"The best politics is right action."

~ Mahatma Gandhi

"Behold a candle, how it gives its light.
It weeps its life away drop by drop in order
to give forth its flame of light."

~ Abju'l-Baha

"The unendurable is the beginning of
the curve of joy."

~ Djuna Barnes

"...The heart is truly a transnational organ...how necessary it is that one learns to feel the heart not as one's own, but as something that belongs to the entire world."

~ *Agni Yoga Teaching*

"Be gentle with the earth."

~ *Dalai Lama*

"I offer you peace.
I offer you love.
I offer you friendship.
I see your beauty.
I hear your need.
I feel your feelings.
My wisdom flows from the Highest Source.
I salute that Source in you.
Let us work together for unity and love."

~ *Mahatma Gandhi, Prayer for Peace.*

"Do not take yourself so seriously, and you will find that you will release yourself for freer and more potent work."

~ *Alice A. Bailey*

"Your prime purpose on earth is to help one another. If you can't help one another at least don't hurt one another."

~ *Dalai Lama*

"Cease to identify yourselves with material things or with your desires, gain a proper sense of value; cease regarding possessions and earthly existence as of major importance; follow the Noble Eightfold Path which is the Path of Right Relations…and thus be Happy."

~ The Buddha

"Love is the very foundation, beauty and fulfillment of life. If we dive deep enough into ourselves, we will find that the one thread of universal love ties all beings together. As this awareness dawns within us, peace alone will reign."

~ *Mata Amritanandamayi*

"The heart is considered the palace of the imagination. How is it possible to move forward if the power of imagination is missing? But where will imagination come from, if not from experience?"

~ *Agni Yoga Teaching*

"The most beautiful people we have known are those who have known defeat, known suffering, known struggle, known loss, and have found their way out of the depths. These persons have an appreciation, a sensitivity and an understanding of life that fills them with compassion, gentleness, and a deep loving concern. Beautiful people do not just happen."

~ Elizabeth Kubler-Ross

"Ye shall know the truth,
and the truth shall make you free."

~ John 8:32

"If you do not change direction,
you may end up where you are heading."

~ Lao Tzu

"Across the deserts, seas, and mountains,
You transport yourselves in one breath.
And there, face to face, we meet.
There is no space. Time exists not.
The power of knowledge is manifested...
Sour with your thoughts. Fly by affirmation.
Fly by love."

~ *Agni Yoga Society*

"Skip religion and the politics, head straight for the compassion. Everything else is a distraction."

~ *Talib Kweli*

"Kindness is the mark of faith, and whoever has not kindness has not faith."

~ *Muhammad*

"The things we now esteem fixed shall, one by one, detach themselves like ripe fruit from our experience and fall…The Soul looketh steadily forwards, creating a world before her, leaving worlds behind her."

~ Ralph Waldo Emerson

"In some way, suffering ceases to be suffering at the moment it finds meaning."

~ *Friedrich Nietzsche*

"Galadriel: 'Mithrandir, why the Halfling?' Gandalf: 'I do not know. Saruman believes that it is only great power that can hold evil in check. But that is not what I've found. I've found it is the small things, every act of normal folk that keeps the darkness at bay—simple acts of kindess and love. Why Bilbo Baggins? Perhaps it is because I am afraid and he gives me courage.'"

~ *The Hobbit:*
An Unexpected Journey

"The future does have a name, and its name is Hope."

~ *Pope Francis*

"How do we get closer to this genuine spiritual self? By manifesting love and compassion. Why? Because love and compassion are far more than the abstractions many of us believe them to be. They are real. They are concrete. And they make up the very fabric of the spiritual realm. In order to return to that realm, we must once again become like that realm, even while we are stuck in, and plodding through, this one."

~ *Dr. Eben Alexander*

"My head is bursting with the joy of the unknown. My heart is expanding a thousand fold."

~ *Rumi*

"How much more could we achieve if we have the right mindset to make the world better?"

~ *Rowlands Kaotcha*

"Love is an endless mystery, for it has nothing else to explain it."

~ *Rabindranath Tagore*

Did you find inspiration for yourself in this book?

I'd love to hear about it!

Please email me at SusanMacNeilphd@gmail.com

or visit my website at www.PsychologywithaSoul.com.

Made in the USA
Columbia, SC
13 March 2018